T0284195

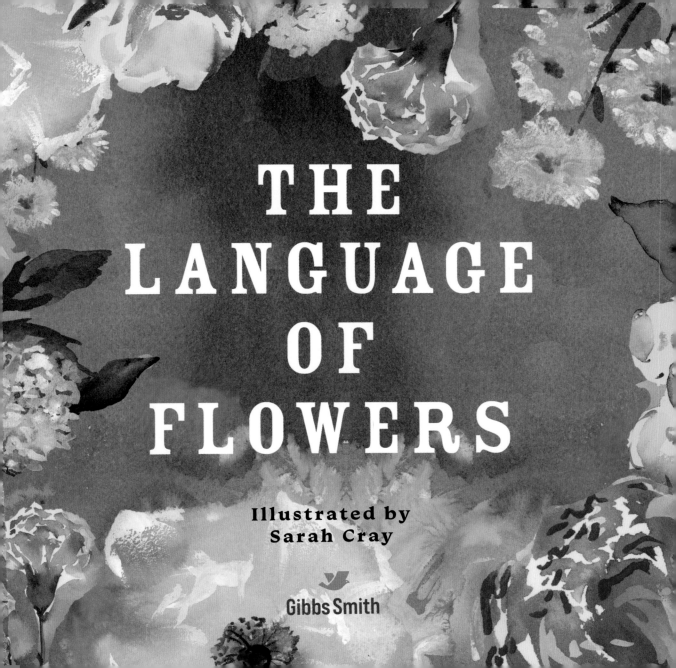

THE
LANGUAGE
OF
FLOWERS

Illustrated by
Sarah Cray

Gibbs Smith

4

INTRODUCTION

———

When we stop to admire a flower, we take in its lovely scent or elegant form. But what most of us don't know is that there is a language of flowers, and this language is filled with symbolism. In the pages ahead, you'll be able to explore some of the most beautiful flowers and the messages we send with each bouquet.

BIRD-OF-PARADISE

freedom, joy, excitement

The bird-of-paradise is named for its striking appearance. When the bright orange and blue petals bloom, they resemble a tropical bird in flight. With a long stem that reaches toward the heavens, this flower is a reminder that heaven on Earth can exist.

CAMELLIA

devotion, love, refinement

When the petals of a flower fall off, the leafy part usually remains. But when the camellia wilts, its petals and leaves fall away together. That is why it is said to represent devotion and enduring love between two people, even after death.

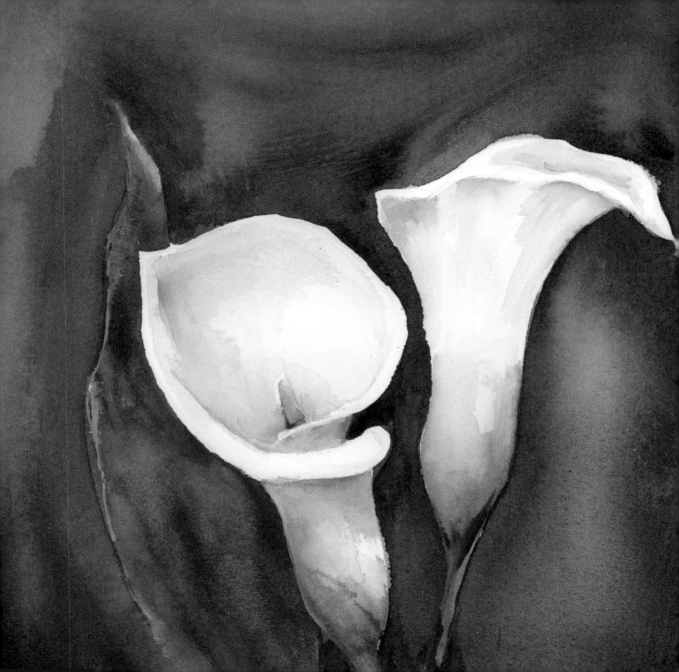

CALLA LILY

beauty, fertility, rebirth

Known for its breathtaking elegance, the calla lily has been a symbol of beauty since ancient times. In Greek mythology, it is attributed to the goddess Hera. Calla lilies are commonly used in Easter services and have come to symbolize rebirth or resurrection.

LAVENDER

serenity, grace, calm

Lavender's name comes from the Latin word for "bathing" because it was used for washing and cleaning in ancient Rome. The gentle scent of lavender promotes calm and relaxation, so the flower is often an expression of tranquility.

SUNFLOWER

positivity, happiness, loyalty

———————

These flowers turn their large, round faces toward the sun, making them a popular symbol of optimism and joy. Sunflowers are also associated with loyalty and consistency. This is reflected in the way their heads follow the sun across the sky.

SWEET WILLIAM

masculinity, gallantry, courage

———

Tales say the name of this flower honors William Shakespeare or Prince William, the eighteenth-century Duke of Cumberland. Duchess Kate had sweet William in her wedding bouquet, and many lovelorn young men in English folkloric ballads, such as "Fair Margaret and Sweet William," use the name.

POINSETTIA

success, good cheer, purity

This bloom's starry leaf pattern symbolizes the Star of Bethlehem, closely associating poinsettias with Christmas. When given as a gift, they offer wishes of success, positivity, and good luck in the coming year.

QUEEN ANNE'S LACE

safety, refuge, peace

The delicate, lacelike flowers of this bloom resemble the shape of an umbrella or a bird's nest. This is likely why it is seen as a symbol of sanctuary and protection.

ZINNIA

endurance, friendship, remembrance

———

Zinnias are a way to say goodbye or pay tribute to someone who is important. The colorful blossoms are symbols of affection, but they also represent longevity due to their resilient and sturdy nature.

PRIMROSE

young love, femininity

These flowers are recognized in Norse mythology as a symbol of Freya, the goddess of love. During the Victorian era, primrose signified youth and young love. A gift of primrose was said to mean "I can't live without you." Primrose is also attributed to femininity and womanhood.

ALSTROEMERIA

unity, stability, devotion

———————

Commonly known as Peruvian lily, this flower is sacred to the Inca. It has three petals and three sepals, comprising six distinct parts that each represent a different characteristic: commitment, empathy, humor, patience, respect, and understanding. The leaves twist together to form a symbol of bonding and unity.

DAHLIA

creativity, commitment, appreciation

Dahlias have held significance across different cultures throughout history. The ancient Aztecs used them in religious ceremonies. In the Victorian era, people gave dahlias to their loved ones as a symbol of lifelong commitment. Today, they are often associated with inner strength and creativity because of their bold, vivid appearance.

GARDENIA

purity, beauty, hope

Gardenias are most commonly found in white, which has led them to be associated with purity and clarity. In France, men have traditionally worn them as boutonnières to express pure intentions as a suitor. Their white color also represents a blank canvas upon which hopes and dreams can be projected.

T U L I P

love, charity

O ver centuries, tulips have endured as a symbol of love. They are native to Persia, and their name is thought to derive from the Persian word for "turban." The tulip's most common meaning is unconditional love.

POPPY

sleep, peace, death

Due to the opium extracted from them and their bloodred color, poppies have long been associated with sleep and death. Around the world, red poppies are commonly worn on Remembrance Day to commemorate those who died in war.

LOTUS

beauty, resilience, respect

The lotus flower grows in dark, swampy areas but blossoms into a spectacular flower when it reaches the light. This makes it a symbol of enlightenment and growth, especially in Eastern cultures and religions. In Hinduism and Buddhism, the lotus is considered sacred.

VIOLET

modesty, humility, faith

I n Christianity, the violet represents the modesty of the Virgin Mary. Its delicate petals, gentle appearance, and pleasing scent symbolize innocence and humility.

WILD ROSE

beauty, love, secrets

Aphrodite, the Greek goddess of love and beauty, is represented by the wild rose. These flowers are symbols of infatuation and desire. Historically, they have also been an emblem of secrecy. Wild roses were placed over church confessionals to represent confidentiality.

MAGNOLIA

strength, endurance, connection

The magnolia tree is strong and majestic, with white flowers that mean everlasting connection. They also represent dignity and grace. Different colors of magnolia each hold their own significance: White flowers mean purity, pink flowers mean joy, purple flowers mean good luck, and green flowers mean good fortune.

MARIGOLD

passion, happiness, optimism

———

Marigolds open up and bloom when the sun rises. Their pleasant, round appearance and association with the sun bring out positive energy. These golden flowers are symbols of happiness, optimism, and warmth.

FORGET-ME-NOT

respect, love, faithfulness

A lthough small and delicate, the forget-me-not is a powerful symbol of love and fidelity. Giving someone these tiny blooms is a way of saying you will always remember them. It is also a token of remembrance for those who have parted.

GLADIOLUS

sincerity, honor, remembrance

———

Gladiolus is a bloom that represents strength of character. The name comes from the word "gladius," a Latin word for "sword," because of its long, pointed shape. In ancient Rome, the flower was associated with gladiators.

RED ROSE

love, passion, union

———

There is no greater expression of romantic love than the red rose. From a single stem to a large bouquet, the number of roses that are given to someone bears significance. One red rose can mean love at first sight. Three red roses are traditionally a one-month anniversary gift. A dozen red roses is a classic, timeless declaration of love.

SNAPDRAGON

virtue, grace, protection

Ancient cultures were fascinated by the snapdragon's distinct look and ability to grow in rocky terrain. Considered a symbol of feminine strength and grace, snapdragons are often given as a show of respect or admiration.

ORCHID

fertility, elegance

As a symbol of beauty, the orchid has long been an object of fascination and desire. The flower's elegant, graceful appearance and intricate details showcase the majesty of nature. Orchids are a symbol of love, fertility, and luxury.

FREESIA

friendship, trust, thoughtfulness

In Victorian times, people used freesias to pass secret messages to each other. This is why they are considered a sign of trust. Freesias have since become popular in wedding bouquets to symbolize trust between the couple.

CARNATION

affection, young love, fascination

———————

Renaissance painters featured carnations in engagement scenes, and they are closely associated with wedding nuptials. The carnation is the traditional flower used to celebrate a couple's first anniversary. It can also represent familial love or friendship.

DANDELION

happiness, youth, healing

Many of us have childhood memories of dandelions, blowing their seeds away in the wind. As such, they are associated with youth and happiness. The flowers have also been used for medicinal purposes, symbolizing hope and healing.

YUCCA

purity, loyalty, protection

The powdery white flowers of the yucca thrive in the desert, where they recycle the air around them. This is thought to contribute to its meaning of purity. Yucca also means protection, loyalty, and opportunity.

RHODODENDRON

appreciation, love, friendship

The meanings of the rhododendron are characterized by warm feelings because they grow in sunny places. These flowers are symbols of light and positivity. Rhododendrons are often featured in bouquets designed to express love and appreciation.

IRIS

eloquence, nobility, hope

Irises have been a source of inspiration in many different cultures. The flower was featured on the scepters of Egyptian pharaohs to convey power. It also inspired the fleur-de-lis, a symbol used in French heraldry. In general, the iris is admired for its eloquence.

PEONY

love, marriage, prosperity

A perennial, the exquisite peony is a long-lasting flower. Its ability to stand the test of time is why it has long been a symbol of a happy marriage and prosperity. Peonies have a rich, romantic appearance, which is another reason for their popularity in wedding bouquets.

DELPHINIUM

goodwill, positivity, adventure

———

The showy flower spikes of the delphinium stand tall and don't droop, reminding us to keep a positive outlook. Delphiniums scatter their seeds far and wide, so they are also symbols of adventure.

BUTTERCUP

youth, happiness, charm

———

Commonly associated with children, the buttercup has a whimsical air of youth and playfulness. This sense of joy is also conveyed through its bright, happy appearance. Buttercups symbolize charm and likability.

JASMINE

beauty, sensuality, modesty

Jasmine's delicate appearance and sweet, rich fragrance are thought to evoke sensuality and romance. Because the small flowers on some species only bloom at night, jasmine can also represent modesty.

CHRYSANTHEMUM

joy, longevity, optimism

Because chrysanthemums bloom in fall, they are known for providing joy and color despite the impending winter. Different varieties each hold their own significance. Red symbolizes love and passion, yellow symbolizes loss or grief, and white symbolizes loyalty.

HEATHER

good luck, protection, confidence

———————

A sprig of heather is traditionally thought to bring good luck and protection. In Scotland, it is common for heather to be added to a bridal bouquet for this reason. Because it can grow in tough places, heather can also represent confidence and independence.

GERANIUM

happiness, friendship

The geranium flower has held significance across many cultures, often being associated with gods and saints. In Victorian times, different scents of geranium were said to convey different meanings. Overall, the flower is considered a symbol of happiness and friendship.

BLUEBELL

humility, gratitude, everlasting love

Bluebells appear in tales from folklore, often in a magical and enchanting way. Many superstitions surround this graceful flower, one of which says you will find true love if you can turn the flower inside out without tearing it.

BEGONIA

caution, vigilance, respect

The begonia has traditionally served as an omen or warning of future misfortune. In some cultures, this message of caution is delivered when you give a begonia to someone. It is a way of telling them to take care and stay well.

LILY OF THE VALLEY

happiness, purity

Lily of the valley is a delicate, fragrant bloom that signifies a return to happiness. Its scientific name means "belonging to May." Giving someone a bunch of lilies of the valley during that month is a way to express a meaningful connection and to spread happiness.

CROCUS

new beginnings, positivity

Crocus flowers bloom in early spring, bringing much-needed cheer after a long winter. They symbolize fresh starts, rebirth, and a general sense of positivity. In ancient Greece, the vines of the crocus were woven together as garlands for wedding decorations.

HYDRANGEA

gratitude, honesty, abundance

———

Hydrangeas are linked to sincere, heartfelt emotions like gratitude and compassion. They are often used to express thanks or understanding. Due to their round blooms with ample flowers, they can also mean abundance and wealth.

HIBISCUS

beauty, femininity, opportunity

Hibiscus flowers bloom for only one day before they close and eventually fall off the vine. Due to this short span in which it flashes its gorgeous colors, the hibiscus represents ephemeral beauty. It is also a reminder to seize opportunities since they could be gone in a flash.

LILAC

renewal, confidence, romance

Due to their early blooming season, lilacs are symbols of springtime and rebirth. They are also associated with confidence, so lilacs are often given as graduation gifts. The flower has been admired for its sweet scent throughout history and has therefore been closely associated with romantic love.

DAFFODIL

honesty, faithfulness, forgiveness

———————

Daffodils are renowned for their ease and reliability. They return to bloom in spring, year after year, which is why they symbolize faithfulness. In some cultures, daffodils are an auspicious sign of good fortune.

APPLE BLOSSOM

love, sensuality, endurance

Apple flowers and fruits were regarded as a symbol of love in Celtic culture. Ancient Celts would adorn their bedchambers with apple blossoms to induce a romantic evening. The apple blossom also represents long life.

DAISY

purity, innocence

The name daisy is said to be a variation of "day's eye" because the flower closes its head every night and opens up again in the morning. Different meanings are ascribed to different colors of this gentle, cheerful bloom. White daisies represent purity, pink daisies represent romance, and yellow daisies represent happiness or friendship.

HYACINTH

forgiveness, sorrow, peace

Purple hyacinth symbolizes regret and has traditionally been used to ask for forgiveness. A bouquet of purple hyacinth is a way to offer an apology. The flower comes in a variety of colors, with more positive meanings that range from playfulness to peace to commitment.

STARGAZER LILY

success, prosperity

Unlike many other lilies, the Stargazer variety grows upright as if looking toward the starry sky. This show of vitality contributes to its meaning of success and fulfilled dreams.

ASTER

wisdom, valor, elegance

Named after the Greek word for "star," this bloom symbolizes wisdom and courage. In ancient times, asters were laid on the graves of French soldiers who had died in battle. Today, the starlike flowers are a symbol of love and elegance.

PANSY

platonic love, admiration, remembrance

Pansies encompass the full range of loving feelings. Although they can symbolize love for a romantic partner, they are commonly associated with the platonic love and affection shared between family and friends. The pansy is also a flower of remembrance, often placed on headstones and memorials.

Sarah Cray is the creator of Dandelion Paper Co. and "Let's Make Art," an online community and art supply shop with the goal of getting more people to paint and live a more creative life. Sarah lives in Hamilton, Missouri, with her family.

FOR ARLO, MY SONSHINE

First Edition
27 26 25 24   5

Text © 2023 Gibbs Smith Publisher
Illustrations © 2023 Sarah Cray

Published by Gibbs Smith
P.O. Box 667
Layton, Utah 84041
1.800.835.4993 orders
www.gibbs-smith.com

Designed by Virginia Snow

Printed and bound in China
Gibbs Smith books are printed on either recycled, 100% post-consumer waste, FSC-certified papers or on paper produced from sustainable PEFC-certified forest/controlled wood source. Learn more at www.pefc.org.

Library of Congress Control Number: 2022944110
ISBN: 978-1-4236-6158-0